HAMLYN · COLOURFAX ·

SNOOKER
Billiards & Pool

IAN MORRISON & TERRY SMITH

CONTENTS

Equipment and rules	2
Grip, stance and bridge	6
Sighting and striking the ball	8
Potting and angles	10
The awkward shots	12
The world of spin	14
Controlling the cue-ball	16
Plants and doubles	18
Breaking off and safety play	20
Snookers and how to escape	22
Trick shots	24
The professional game	26
How to play billiards	28
How to play pool	30
Index	32

HAMLYN

Equipment and rules

INTRODUCTION

Snooker is popularly believed to have started in 1875 at an army camp in India where the officers used to play black pool, with 15 reds, a white and a black ball. One officer started to experiment by adding various coloured balls to the three balls used for billiards. Eventually, it developed into the set-up we know today – 15 reds, yellow, green, brown, blue, pink, black and a white cue-ball.

Snooker is now the most popular sport on television and is played by millions of people – young and old. In this book, you will find all the basics: the equipment you need, the rules and how to play; how to stand properly, the way to hold the cue, the tactics of the game and the shots that will help you win.

Now it is up to you and one day you, too, could be world champion – just like Steve Davis.

THE TABLE

A full-size snooker table measures about 1.83 m (6 ft) wide by 3.66 m (12 ft) long, and this can seem incredibly big to the beginner. There are smaller tables which can fit into the average living room.

The bed of a full size table is formed by five slate slabs. Each weighs about 150 kg (3 cwt) and is about 5 cm (2 in) thick. A full-size table needs eight solid wooden legs. The bed is covered with a tightly-stretched green cloth.

The actual playing area is a little smaller, because it is surrounded by six rubber cushions, so that the balls rebound when they hit them. You can imagine what could happen without them!

The pockets are housed in openings at each of the four corners, and in the middle of the two long sides. This is

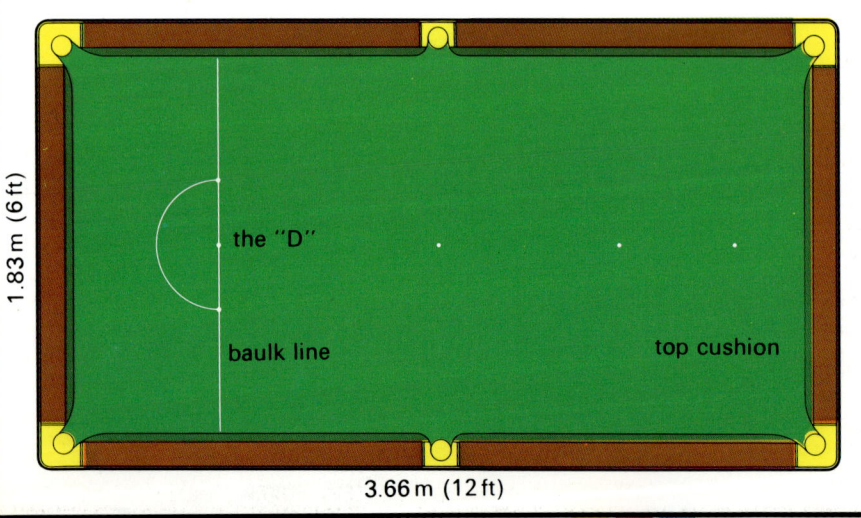

Cues come in one or two pieces, but no matter which you use, keep it chalked regularly and, like these two, enjoy the game!

These are the measurements of a full size table. You'll probably start on a much smaller one. There's a line drawn across the table 73.6 cm (29 in) from the bottom cushion. This divides the table into two unequal parts, and is called the baulk line. This is very important in billiards (but less so in snooker).

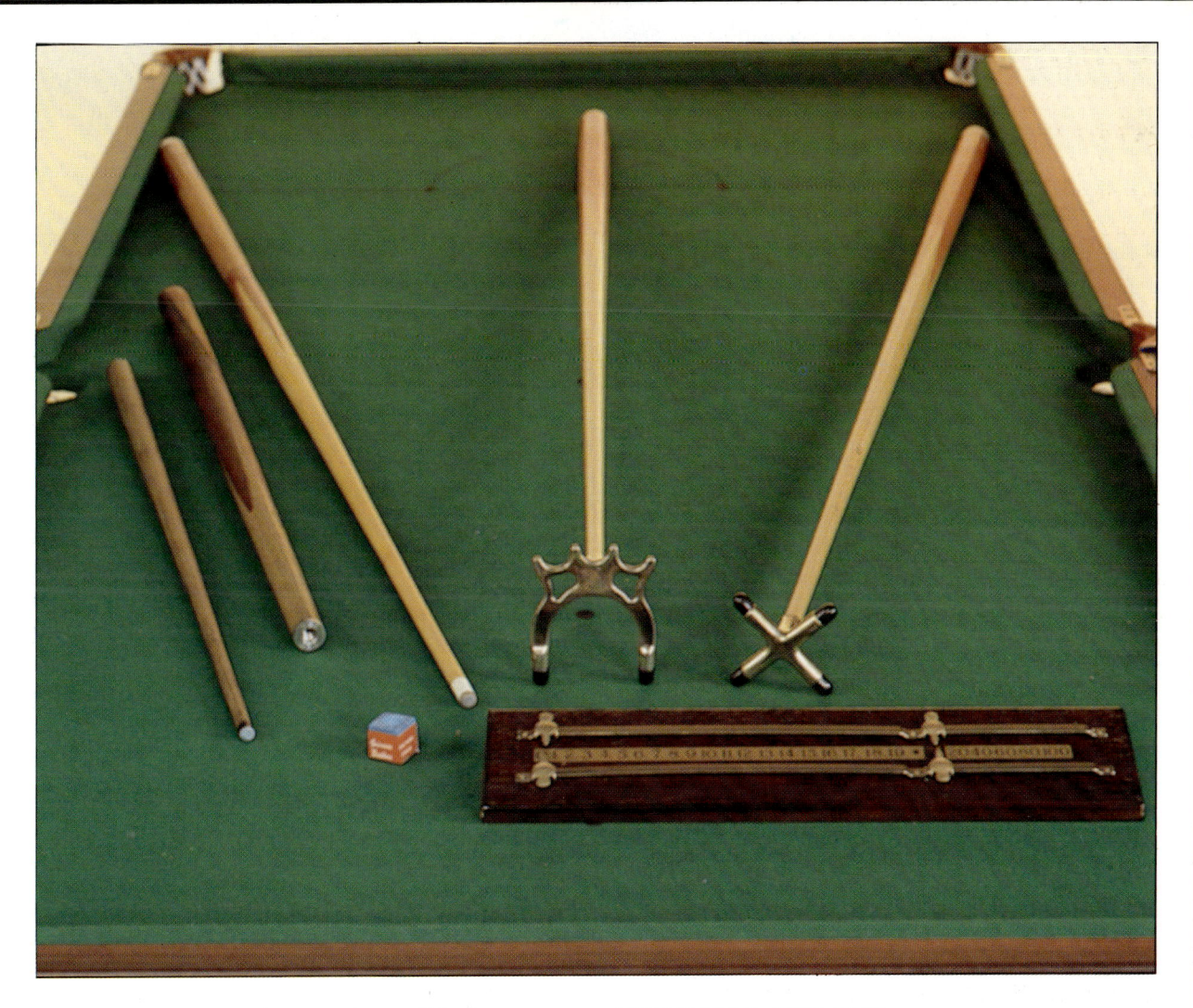

This is the basic equipment that will help get you started. From left to right there is a two-piece cue, a one-piece cue, a spider, and a rest. These generally come with a junior table, but when you advance to a full size table you'll be given a greater choice. In the front there is some chalk and a scoreboard.

where you will try to pot the balls.

There are three spots along the baulk line. On these are placed the green, brown and yellow balls. A semi-circle is drawn from the centre of the baulk line and into the baulk area. This is known as the "D". When playing any shot at the beginning of a game, or when the white has to be played after going off the table or into a pocket, it is brought back into play on any position within the "D".

What do you need apart from a table?

THE BALLS AND CUE

A set of balls, of course. In snooker a full set consists of 15 reds, six colours and a cue-ball (the white). The red balls, when pocketed, are worth 1 point each. Each colour has a different points value: yellow–2, green–3, brown–4, blue–5, pink–6, black–7. Each ball is 52.55 mm ($2\frac{1}{6}$ in) diameter.

Next, you need a cue. Cues are made of wood, and must be a minimum of 91 cm (3 ft) long. The cue is thick at one end, and tapers towards the other. The end you hold is called the butt. The other end has a small tip, and it is this that makes contact with the cue-ball. You must regularly apply special chalk to the tip to prevent the tip miss-hitting the cue-ball. But don't overdo it; you need only a thin

3

EQUIPMENT AND RULES

It's important to stand properly and feel comfortable, but make sure you're properly in line with the shot you're making.

layer. Good players will chalk their cue after every shot.

Cues are made either in one or two pieces. Two-piece cues are joined in the middle but come apart easily and are much easier to carry. A full-size one-piece cue is nearly 1.52 m (5 ft) long.

Since a snooker table has quite a large playing surface, there will be times when you won't be able to reach across it to play a shot. That is when you will need some accessories to help you.

For shots just too far away you will use a *cross-rest* as well as your own cue. If you still cannot reach the ball, you can add a *cue-extension* to the end of your cue. If you still cannot reach the cue-ball, use either the *half-butt* or *long rest*.

Occasionally you will find the cue-ball resting amongst a cluster of balls so that it is impossible to get your hand in to form a bridge for your cue. This is when you might use the *spider*. In some cases, the *extended spider* will have to be used.

And that's about all you need.

THE RULES

Snooker is normally played by two players, although it can be played in pairs. However we will look only at the singles game.

After deciding which player has the first shot, the cue-ball is placed in the "D". The cue-ball is the only one you are allowed to strike with the tip of your cue. The first player attempts to send the white up the table and into the pyramid of reds, without disturbing them too much.

If you pot a red, you receive one point and continue your break by attempting to pot a coloured ball. It is not essential to pot a colour but if you don't, your break ends, and your opponent plays next. A break also comes to an end if you play a foul stroke.

If you successfully pot a colour after a red, you receive the points value of the coloured ball added to your one point for the red. Play then continues and you attempt another red, and so on until the break ends. All reds potted stay in the pocket, but the coloured balls are brought back on to the table and placed on their spot. If their own spot is not available, they go on the highest-value spot that is.

Once all 15 reds have been potted, the colours have to be potted in sequence according to their value, starting with the lowest (yellow) through to the highest (black). Once all balls have been pocketed, the game comes to an end and the player with the most points is the winner. If you feel at any time that you cannot possibly score enough to win the frame, you can concede to your opponent.

If the scores are level at the end of the frame, the black is brought back up and put back on its spot, and the players

Don't be frightened of playing with the spider and rest – they're there to help you. Without them you would struggle to play the shot, but be careful not to disturb other balls with them. You would be committing a foul.

decide by the toss of a coin who shall play first. Play starts again with the white in the "D". The first person to pot the black is the winner. Alternately, if a player commits a foul on the black, he loses.

If you are playing with a friend, it is fair for the better player to give his opponent a start. This makes the game more enjoyable as well as more fair. If you are, say, 21 points better than your opponent, give him a start equivalent to that: it will also improve your own game.

FOULS

All fouls are worth a minimum of 4 points, but will be worth more if the value of the ball "on"(that is the one you are trying to pot), or the ball "fouled" has a points value greater than 4.

There are many ways in which you can commit a foul. The most common are:
1 putting the white into a pocket
2 hitting the wrong ball with the cue-ball
3 failing to hit a ball at all
4 failing to have one foot on the floor when making a shot
5 knocking a ball off the table
6 playing a ball while it is moving

Grip, stance and bridge

The most important thing to remember when you start to play snooker is: you must feel comfortable and relaxed.

The most important piece of equipment is your cue, but it is no good if you don't know how to use it properly.

HOLDING THE CUE

There are no set rules about the way to hold the cue. You must feel comfortable, but, more important, you should be in complete control of the cue.

Few top players hold the cue in the same way. However, nearly all of them agree that the best way to obtain control is to hold the butt with most pressure applied by your thumb and first two fingers. The other two fingers should rest gently against the end.

When you are playing a shot, the only part of your body that should move is the arm holding the cue. The cueing arm should always be kept straight. The tendency for a beginner is to allow the elbow to point away from the body. Watch Steve Davis from behind. His elbow and

Hold the cue as near the end as possible – at least no more than about 7.5 cm (3 in) from the end. Keep your chin down and keep your eyes on the ball.

cueing arm remain in a straight line with the shot. As a result the shot moves smoothly and without swaying from side-to-side. Unless you can learn how to play a stroke in one smooth action, then you can't expect the cue-ball to do what you want.

Now you can hold the cue, how, and where, do you stand?

Lining up the shot (left) *and having completed the stroke* (right). *Note how the head is kept down and the eyes kept on the balls. Don't lift your head immediately after playing the stroke.*

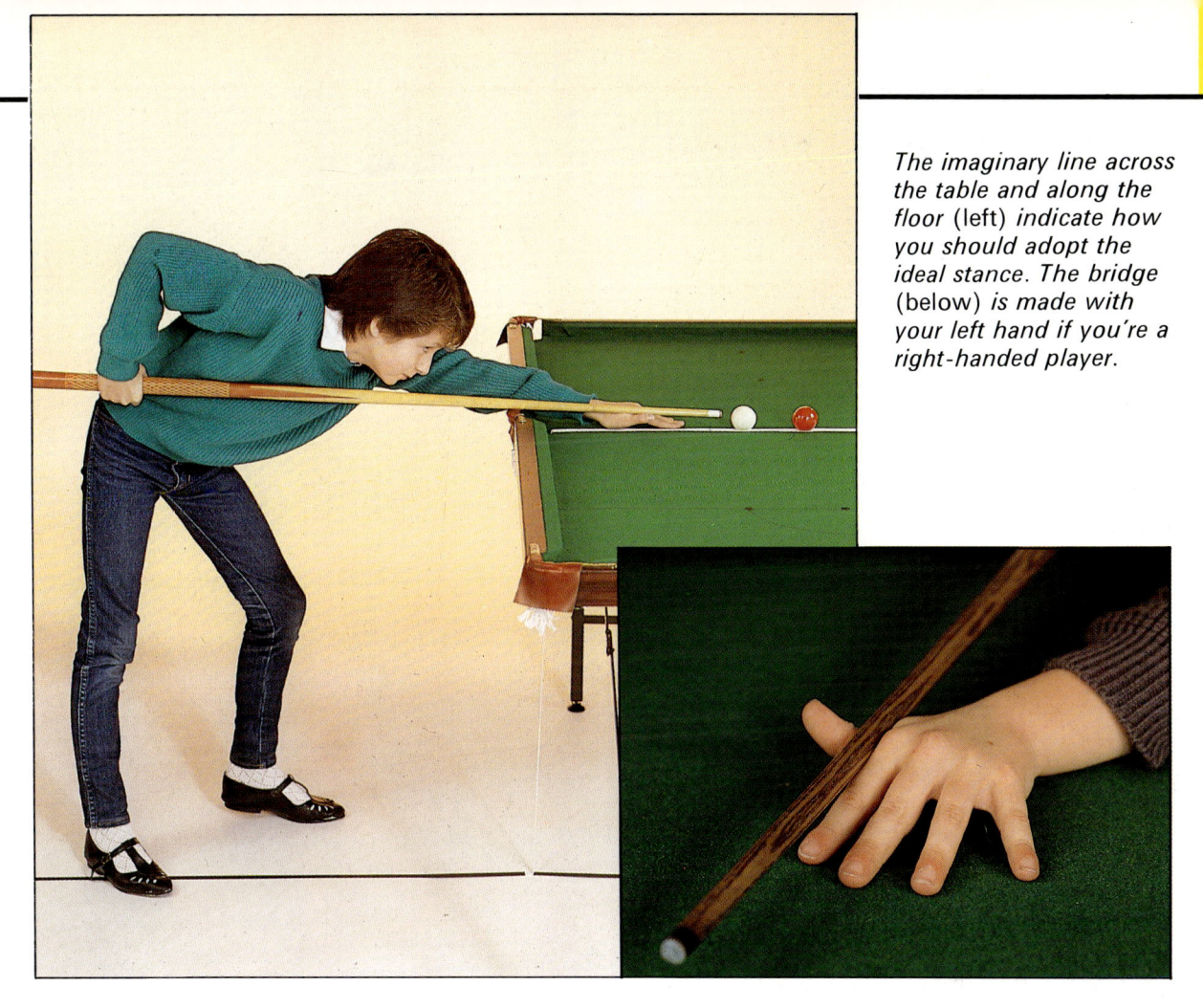

The imaginary line across the table and along the floor (left) *indicate how you should adopt the ideal stance. The bridge* (below) *is made with your left hand if you're a right-handed player.*

STANCE

First, you must always have at least part of one foot on the floor when making every shot. Again, comfort is very important.

Place your feet, as shown in the photograph, with your right foot on a line with the cue-ball, but at a slight angle. The left leg should be forward and should be slightly bent at the knee. Weight should be equally distributed between both feet.

Place your left arm flat and straight on the table. Put your head well down and as near as possible to the cue, without touching it with your chin. Your eyes should look down the cue at the cue-ball. Do not lift your head until after you have completed your shot. Many beginners are tempted to lift their heads before the shot is finished – don't!

Finally, the bridge is formed by the hand controlling the tip end of your cue. Even if you can hold the cue properly, stand correctly and comfortably, it is pointless if the cue is going to wander all over the place as you attempt to play your shot. It is extremely important that you have a good bridge.

THE BRIDGE

The bridge is formed with your left hand. Place it flat on the table, fingers slightly apart, raise your thumb and then pull your fingers towards you while gripping the cloth. Your raised thumb should then have created a perfect "V" in which to position the cue. It is this "V" that decides how good your bridge is. Make sure it is not too tight. If it is, the cue will not move smoothly.

Spend time trying to get your grip, bridge and stance right. You will be able to develop your playing skills as time goes by, but once you have developed a bad stance, grip, or bridge, it is almost impossible to change them.

SIGHTING AND STRIKING THE BALL

We will look at the effect of spin later on, but first let's concentrate on learning how to hit the cue-ball in the centre.

As you look down the cue you see the cue-ball. If you have made a good bridge and your potting arm is moving fluently, then, once you have lined up the tip of your cue with the middle of the cue-ball, you should have no problems. That is the point the cue will hit the ball. If it doesn't

Look at the diagram on the right. Imagine another ball, the black for example, touching the red and in a direct line to the pocket as shown. No matter from where you played another ball, if it hit the black, the red would go in the pocket. This is because the black was in contact with the point of aim on the red.

In the diagram on the far right you are trying to pot the red, but this time the

When lining up your shot, get into the habit of looking at first the cue-ball and then the object ball.

There are many parts of the cue-ball you can strike, but as a beginner learn to make contact with the middle.

then something is wrong, and you must find out why before you go any further.

Once you feel confident that you will strike the ball in the correct place, don't worry any longer about it. We go on to the next problem: how to get the cue-ball to hit the object ball (say a red) at the best place. That is: "At the point of aim", but how do you work our where that should be?

black ball has gone. All you have to do is play the cue-ball so it "replaces" the black. In other words, it makes contact with the red at the same point of aim as the black touched it.

Provided your cue-ball makes contact with the red at the same point of aim then the red will go in the pocket. So before you get set to play your shot: determine the point of aim of the object ball.

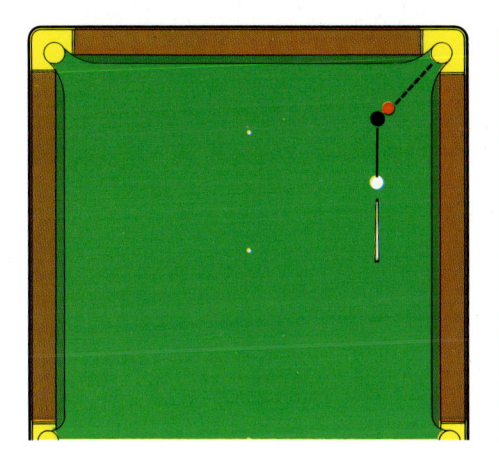

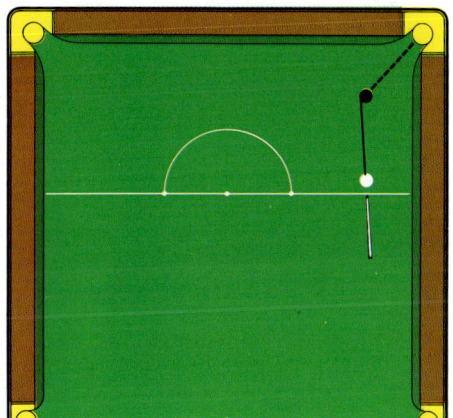

To find the point of aim, mentally picture the black set up for the plant. When you then play your shot the cue-ball should "replace" the black and make contact with the red as shown here.

SIGHTING THE BALL

But where should you sight? Having established the point of aim, you should line up the shot by taking your eyes from the cue-ball to the object ball and back, a few times. Once you are happy you have everything lined up, take your eyes from the cue-ball to the object ball at the last second, and firmly fix them on the point of aim. There is no need to look at the cue-ball because you have got your bridge right, and your cueing action right. So the cue will hit the cue-ball in the centre.

Many younger players take their eyes off the ball too early to see where their shot is going. Resist that temptation. It is a good habit to try and keep your eyes fixed on the object ball longer than necessary. It won't do any harm.

Now try playing a couple of shots with your eyes closed when practising! After all, if you have your cueing and bridging right, once you have established the point of aim there is no reason why the balls should not make the right contact and the red will go in the pocket.

When striking the ball, the shot is lined up with the cue parallel to the table, (top). As it makes contact it remains in the same position (centre). It should also stay in the same position for the follow-through (bottom).

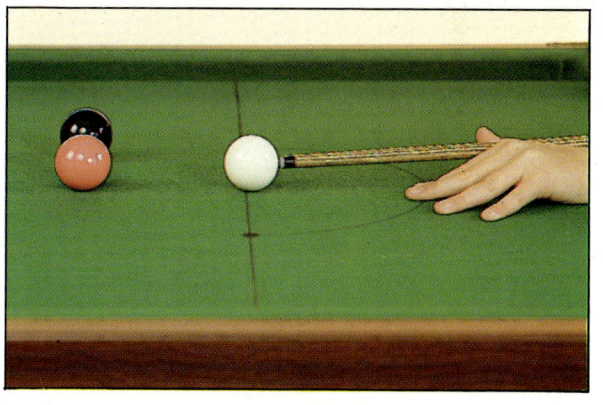

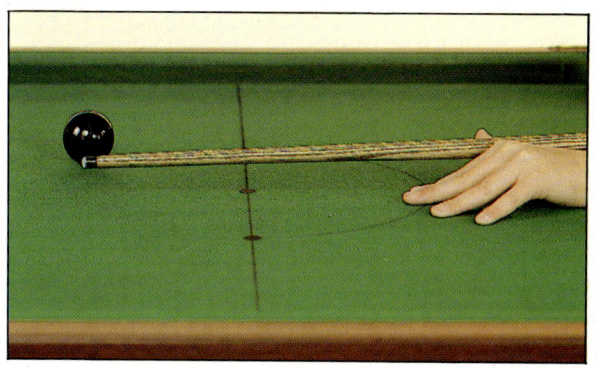

POTTING AND ANGLES

Being able to pot balls is vital. You may hear the expression that playing snooker well is not only being able to pot. As you will see later, it isn't, but if you can't pot, then don't have any ambitions about being world champion.

You must also be able to work out angles.

You have learnt how to work out the point of aim on the object ball, but what happens if you hit it anywhere else?

UNDERSTANDING ANGLES

Let us look at some common snooker shots: the half-ball, the three-quarter ball, and the fine cut. Once you understand these, potting should become easy.

The *half-ball* shot is one of the basic shots of snooker. Know how to play the half-ball, and you are well on your way to understanding angles.

The half-ball shot is the only shot where the angle can be clearly defined. If you play the shot correctly, the object ball will leave its position at an angle of 30°. To play it, the right-edge (or left-edge) of the cue-ball should be in line with the centre of the object ball.

To practise the half-ball shot, set the balls up as shown in the diagram below. If you are playing the shot properly, the red will go in the pocket every time. If it doesn't, then you must be doing something wrong. Start by considering your stance, grip and bridge. If they seem correct, check whether you are hitting the cue-ball in the centre. If you are, check you are keeping your eye on the point of aim for long enough.

Keep practising until the half-ball shot becomes second nature. Once it does, you will be able to make adjustments to cater for intermediate shots such as the three-

This is a nice and easy direct pot. You don't need to work out angles for this one.

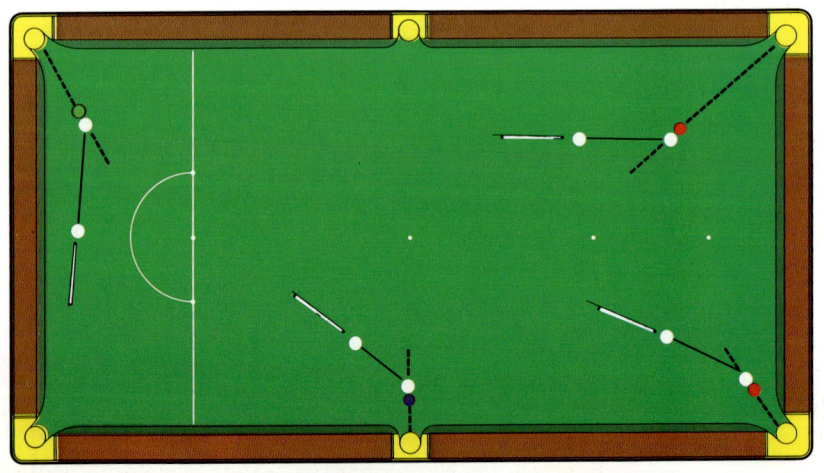

Left: *Some examples to help you to understand angles. In all cases you have to picture a straight line drawn from the pocket through, and beyond, the object ball. The cue-ball should make contact with the object ball at the point where it would be positioned on that line if making a plant.*

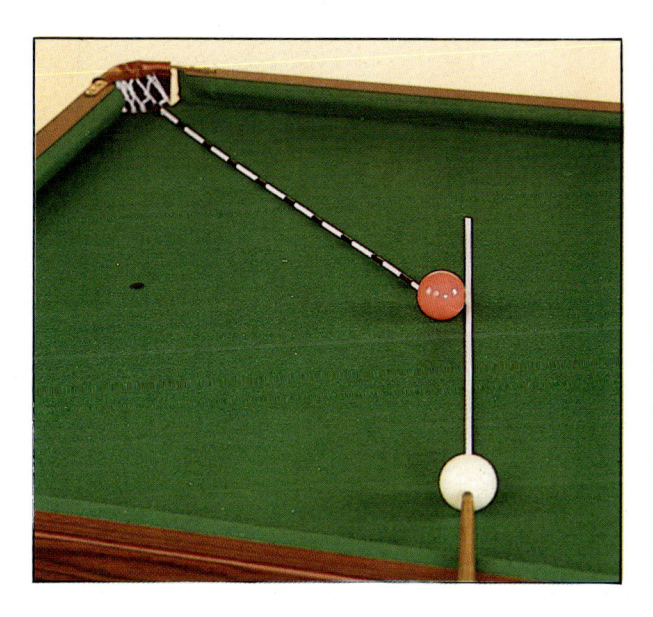

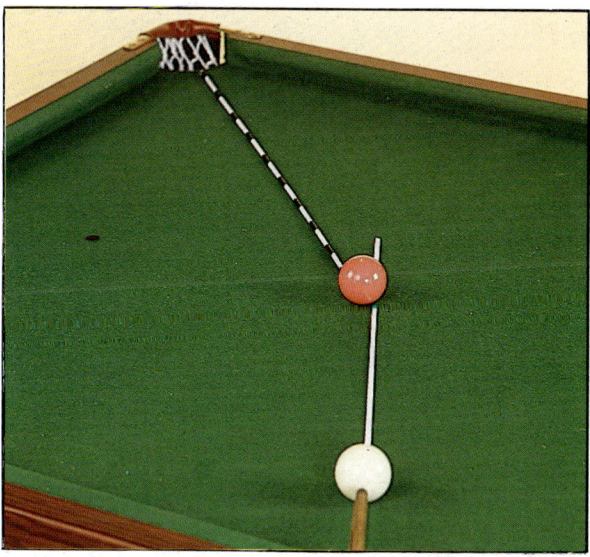

The half-ball shot (above) – *one of snooker's basic shots. If you follow the path of the white its left edge will make contact with the middle of the object ball* (right). *This is the three-quarter ball, so called because the white makes contact with three-quarters of the object ball.*

quarter ball, quarter-ball, or even one-eighth ball, or anything in between.

To see how the angle varies with other shots, have a close look at the *three-quarter ball* shot. This time, the edge of the cue-ball should be in line with a point half-way between the middle and the left edge of the object ball. If you look at the picture, you will see how the direction the object ball travels is very different from that of the half-ball shot.

Once you have understood the angles created by balls making contact at different points, potting will become easier.

However, you must also learn the angles at which a ball rebounds off the cushion. Put simply, a ball will rebound off a cushion at the same angle as it hit it. But of course, as we shall see, side hitting the cue-ball off centre (applying side, *see page 14*) will affect the path of a ball after making contact with the cushion. When practising your half-ball shots notice where the cue-ball goes. In that way you will start to appreciate the different angles at which balls leave the cushion.

Finally, the *fine cut* shot. Anything less than a quarter-ball contact is regarded as a cut. To make a fine cut, you have only to graze the outside edge of the object ball with the cue-ball. The danger of playing the fine cut is that if you miss the object ball altogether, you may leave your opponent "set up" for a pot. If the shot is more than half the length of the table away, then leave well alone, unless you are so far in the lead that you can take the risk.

The quarter-ball: this shot is needed when the object ball has to be cut finely into the pocket.

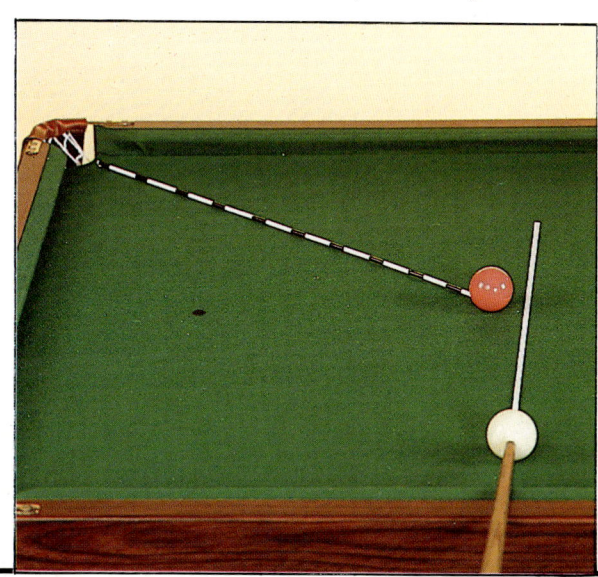

11

THE AWKWARD SHOTS

Not all shots you play are going to be simple. Don't expect that every time you go to the table you will have only to place your left arm on the table, make a nice bridge and play your shot. A good player, if he is not going to be able to make a pot, will always play a safety shot, and leave the cue-ball as close to a cushion as possible. In this way his opponent's next shot will be more difficult. You are going to have to learn to cope with such a situation.

If a ball is close to the cushion, you are restricted in the amount of the ball you can see, and hit. Therefore you have less control over the ball. Players new to the game tend to rush shots on the cushion, because they want to get it over! Don't be misled – it is no different from any other shot, just more awkward.

You should not play down on the ball, but form a bridge with your hand flat on the cushion rail and play in the normal way.

ACCESSORIES

We saw earlier that you are provided with an assortment of accessories to help your game, and now we will look at situations when you are likely to need them.

For those shots that are just too far away, where you cannot make the usual bridge, you will have to use the rest. The end of the rest has a metal or plastic "X" on the end; this replaces the "V" of your bridging hand. Players differ about the way they lay the rest on the table. Some lay it directly under the cue, others to one side. However, the other balls on the table often dictate where you have to put it.

Some shots are more awkward than others because you cannot reach or bridge properly. The rest helps when the ball is too far away to reach. Don't be afraid of it and regard it as your bridge. If the ball is tight on the cushion (below right) you must keep your cue down. Don't lift the butt-end too high (it's a common fault amongst beginners).

One of the game's most awkward pieces of equipment is the spider (left). *It's used for playing a shot when another ball is in front of the cue-ball, preventing you from bridging. Be careful not to touch another ball with your cue or to disturb any other balls as you remove the spider from the table. Below is another way of bridging instead of getting the spider out.*

Never be afraid to use the rest. Many players either through laziness or uncertainty, tend to stretch to make a shot instead of using the cross-rest, and make a complete muddle. During your career as a snooker player, you will often need to use the rest, so get used to it at an early stage and don't be afraid of it.

The "X" on the end has two positions, one for low bridging and one for a slightly higher bridge. Many players make the big mistake of holding the butt of the cue too high when using the rest. You wouldn't hold it high when playing your normal shot would you? So why do it now? Most players prefer to hold their cue between their thumb and first two fingers when playing with the rest. The head of the rest should be about 30–38 cm (12–15 in) from the cue-ball.

If you can't reach the shot with a rest, you should fit the removeable cue-extension to the butt end of your cue.

The half-butt is provided for shots that are about three-quarters the length of the table away. But for those shots that are the full length of the table away, you must use the long rest. Because of their length, both are awkward implements, and come complete with their own cues. If you use either of them, make sure the tips are chalked. The cues on the half-butt and long rest do not need so much power in the shot because of their weight, which adds extra power.

If the cue-ball is surrounded by object balls, then you cannot get in to make a normal bridge. You will either have to attempt to make a high bridge by resting only the tips of your fingers on the table, or use one of the spider rests for cueing over the other balls.

It is your responsibility to remove all accessories from the table. So don't disturb any balls – and remember that it is a foul if you do.

13

THE WORLD OF SPIN

Snooker would certainly be a boring game to watch without the world of spin. We should not appreciate the particular skills of Steve Davis, Jimmy White, Alex Higgins and so on. Fortunately though, spin, with side and screw, have been developed to enhance the game of snooker.

We've said that snooker is not just about potting balls. It is also very important to know what the cue-ball is going to do after it makes contact with an object ball (*see also page 8*). If you can't put spin on a ball, then you will have little control over the cue-ball.

Let's think first about the effects of the different shots.

First, watch the path of a ball struck in the middle and without side or spin. In this case, it will travel straight down the table and back along its own path. Now:

Top spin Playing the ball with top spin will cause it to rotate even further forward and travel further down the table than the previous shot.

If you play the cue-ball with top (left), it will cause it to travel a greater distance around the table after striking the object ball. But playing with bottom (above) will slow down its path after contact.

Bottom spin Striking the ball between the centre and bottom will cause it to rotate in a backwards motion and thus not travel as far as the first ball.

Side spin This time we will play that first ball in the middle, but to the side. Once it makes contact with the cushion this time, it comes off at an angle and takes a different path. If that shot was played with top or bottom spin then it would take the same path, but travel further (with top) or less (with bottom) up the table accordingly.

Screw If you strike the cue-ball near the bottom and follow through with a stab-

THE BALL-CLOCK

The "ball clock" shows where the cue-ball is struck for different spins. Top spin is at 12 o'clock, screw at 6 o'clock, right-hand side at 3 o'clock and left-hand side at 9 o'clock.

To play the screw you lower your bridge. The cue-ball is hit at the bottom and played with a "stabbing" action. After making contact with the object ball it will spin backwards.

bing motion of the cue, it will cause the cue-ball to rotate backwards and, after hitting another ball, will come back along its path.

Stun Similar to the screw, but the cue-ball is hit a bit higher with a stunning motion. This time the cue-ball will stop soon after making contact with another ball.

Running side A ball played near the top and to one side will travel at a wide angle and a long way around the table after making contact with the object ball and cushion.

Check side This is the opposite to running side and the cue-ball is played near the bottom. The cue-ball will "check" its path after hitting a cushion and rebound at a different angle from the one you expect.

These last two shots are complicated. If you can play these, then you're really on your way!

When the cue-ball is played with left-hand side (left), it leaves the cushion at a more acute angle. The same effect is shown below, but this time with right-hand side.

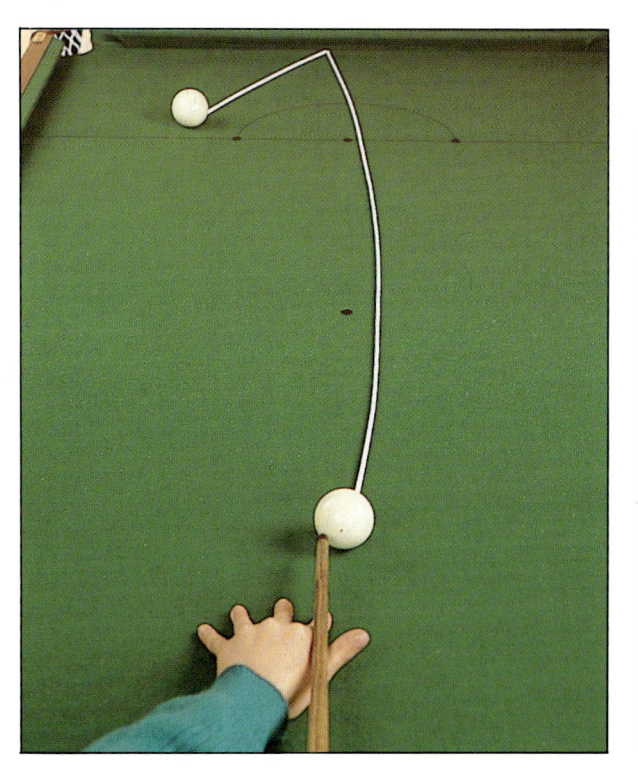

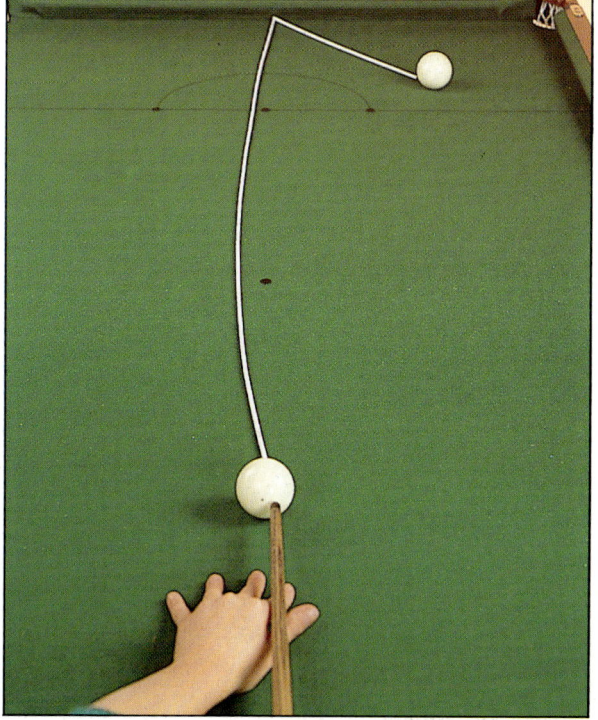

15

CONTROLLING THE CUE-BALL

Potting is one thing, cue-ball control is another. The two go together. A good chess player will be thinking many moves ahead. A good snooker player is no different.

There is no sense in potting a red the full length of the table, only to find the white ending up amongst a cluster of balls and not in a position to hit a colour directly after. Since your next object after potting a red will be to try and pot a colour, you want to make sure the white is in position to make your next task that much easier.

In the pictures shown below and on the right are some examples of the way to play simple shots to make sure you are in position to pot a colour.

It looks easy in a picture, but it is a different story when you are faced with the situation on the table! Experience will only come with practice. You will make mistakes trying to get in the best position. But making mistakes will only help you to learn how *not* to play shots in future.

MORE THAN POTTING

At one time snooker was regarded as less skilful than billiards. But in the 1920s Joe Davis introduced an element of skill never seen before – controlling the cue-ball. Today, none of the leading professionals rely on potting alone – if they did they would certainly not be "leading" professionals. Cue-ball control is all important and you should remember that at all times.

This diagram shows the effect of two different shots that have the same result – that is potting the red and getting on the black. It also shows how you can best use your options. Shot A is the pot played with right hand side on the cue-ball, while shot B is played with a lot of screw on the cue-ball.

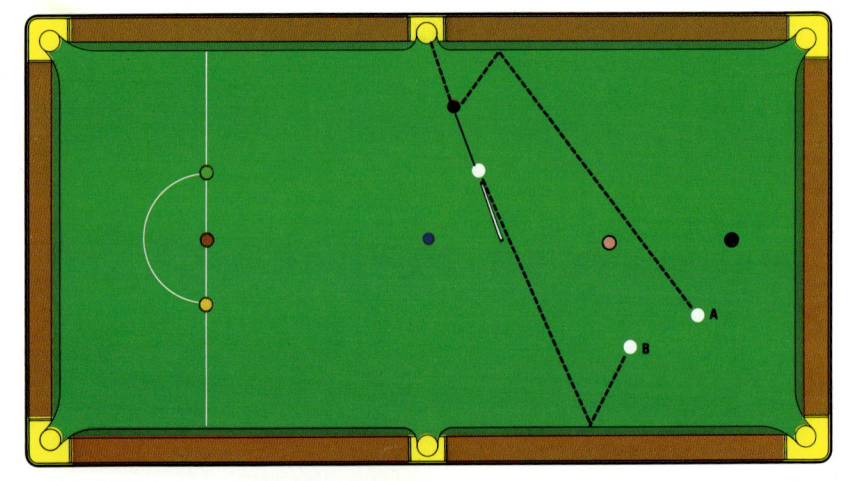

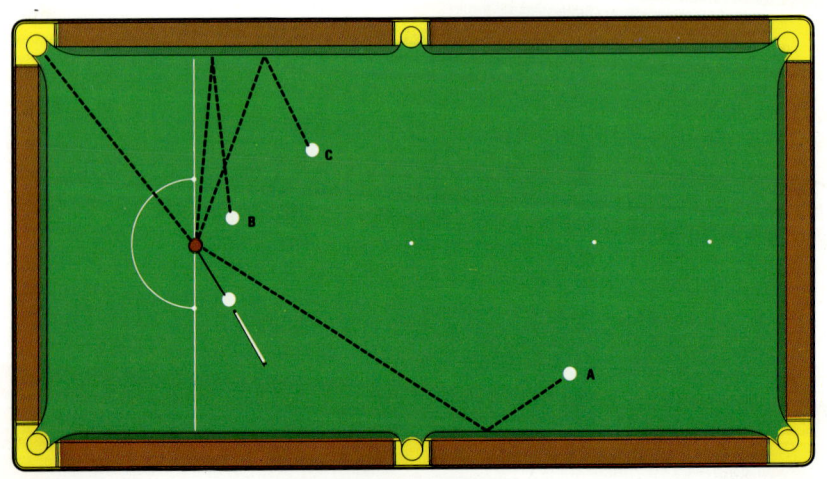

This shot gives you three options to play after the brown, giving you a chance to play a ball at the top, middle or bottom of the table. A is a screw played with a lot of power. B is played with top spin on the cue-ball and C is a stun shot played with some top spin.

You are on the black (right) *but need to get on one of the two reds after making the pot. By playing the cue-ball with some right hand side* (below) *you should finish up with the choice of either red.*

You could easily pot the yellow or the brown, but you have to get on a red with your next shot. Green is therefore going to be your best choice.

By taking the green you now have the perfect angle to make the pot and then come off the side cushion. You should then be in position for the red to go into the middle pocket.

17

Plants and Doubles

Plants and doubles look the most dramatic shots in snooker. Both are more spectacular than the normal pot, that is why audiences applaud when they succeed.

Top players will frequently play a plant, attempting the double less often.

THE DOUBLE

The *double* is a shot that makes the object ball play across the table and into a pocket off a cushion (normally into one of the middle pockets). It is a risky shot because there is every chance that if you miss, it will leave your opponent "set up". There is also the chance of it missing the pocket but hitting the jaws (the entrance to the pocket). It is anybody's guess where it will end up. The double must be played only at the right opportunity.

If you must play it, however, it is best attempted when the object ball is either on, or 2.5 to 5 cm (1–2 in) away from the cushion.

Inexperienced players seem to believe the double has to be played by giving the cue-ball a wallop – it doesn't. If the angle between the two balls is narrow, then a little more power is required to avoid the two balls kissing as the object ball comes off the cushion.

The secret of the successful double is assessing the best angle for the object ball to rebound from the cushion. Stand behind the pocket you are aiming for and look for the point of contact on the cushion which the object ball must hit.

Here are a few doubles to keep you busy. **A** *is risky because of the chance that the two balls will "kiss" because the object ball is close to the cushion.* **B** *is a straightforward double and* **C** *is a reverse double, calling for spot-on accuracy. Lining up a straightforward double is shown below.*

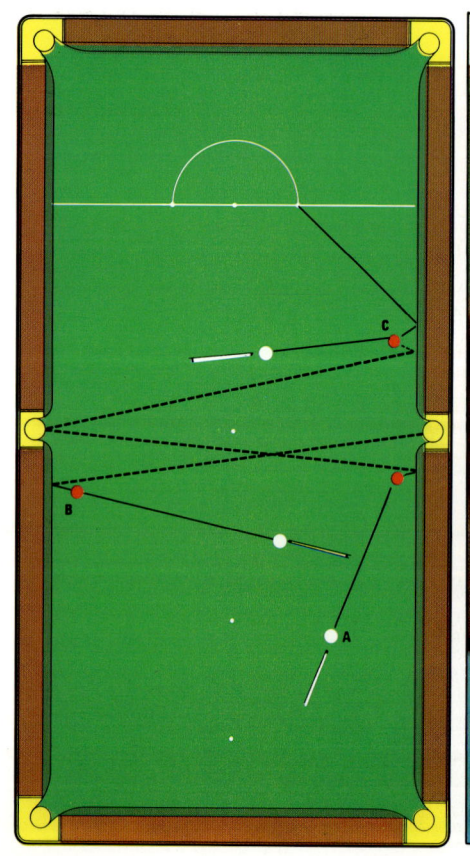

SHOULD I REALLY PLAY THE DOUBLE?

If there is an alternative shot to play then the answer is NO. And quite often there will be another shot to play, but the inexperienced player will still go for the double because it looks good when it goes in.

Remember, there is more chance of playing a good safety shot than a successful double so, if the safety shot is "on" then go for it, and forget about the double.

THE PLANT

The *plant* (or set) is just as dramatic as the double. Yet a plant should rarely be missed – if in doubt, don't try it!

As we saw earlier, when finding the point of aim on the object ball, we placed a black touching the red. On page 8 we said that no matter where the black was hit, the red would go in. That is the same as a plant: two object balls close to or touching each other, so that when the first is struck, the second is potted.

However some plants are more complicated than others. The two object balls may not be touching, or even close together. Occasionally a plant may consist of three, or even more, balls. In some plants one ball has to be played at an angle to play on to and pot another. Those plants are certainly difficult and only an experienced player could succeed. In fact an experienced player would probably not try such a difficult shot at all!

Examples **A** *and* **B** *of these plants are easy to complete whereas* **C** *calls for great accuracy.* **D** *and* **E** *are examples of "in-off" plants. Hit the first red* (below) *and the second red will go in with no problems.*

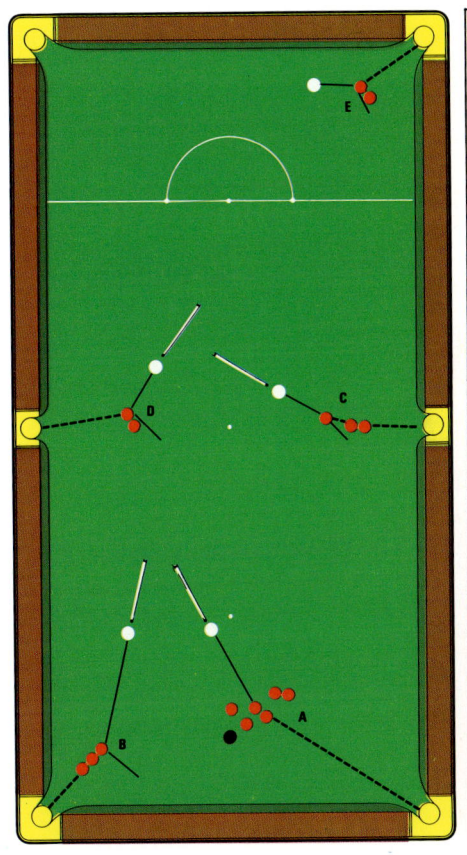

BREAKING OFF AND SAFETY PLAY

The start of the game is very important. If you are breaking, a good break will give you the opening advantage. A bad one will pass that advantage to your opponent.

Many people watching professional snooker find the opening of a frame boring. But even if balls are not being potted the game is still interesting. The opening is like the opening moves in chess as the players play cat-and-mouse waiting for the first mistake.

At the start of the game it is important to be able to break properly, play good safety shots, and understand what a "shot to nothing" shot is. However, the last two points are important parts of your game even after the opening stages.

BREAKING

You will want to hit the white so that it touches the reds but disturbs them as little as possible, and then returns to the baulk area. If you can get the white into baulk, so that it is tight on the cushion or goes behind one of the colours, all the better. Provided you get the white back to baulk, your opponent will have a long distance shot to make as he tries to do the same as you, that is, disturb the reds very little and bring the white back to a safe area.

SAFETY SHOTS

This is where the "cat and mouse" element comes in, and you should always be able to play good *safety shots*. If there is no ball in a potable position, don't take

Breaking off (left). *The view at the start of a game and* (right) *the standard break used by most professionals. This gives the minimum amount of disturbance to the pack of reds, and takes the white into baulk.*

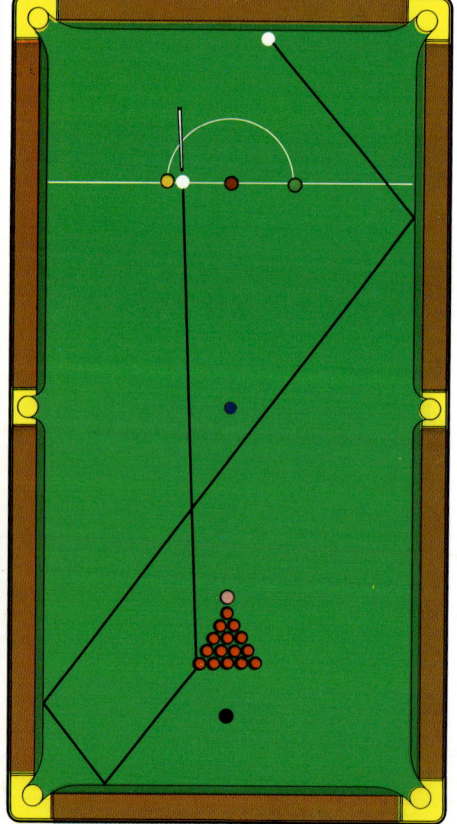

chances. Instead, make contact with it, but don't push it nearer a pocket, and bring the cue-ball to a safe resting place where it is not easy for your opponent to score any points.

There may be a red which you think you can pot, but are not quite sure. You should consider its position, decide what will happen to the cue-ball if the red goes in, and what will happen if it doesn't. If you think the cue-ball will come back to the relative safety of the baulk area, then it is worth attempting the pot. This is called the *shot to nothing*. In other words, you have nothing to lose by trying the pot, and nothing to lose by not making the pot. If you are successful you will find your ball amongst the baulk-end colours.

If, rather than trying to pot one of these colours, you roll the ball up to one instead, you will give yourself a great advantage because your opponent will be "snookered" (*see page 22*). He will have to negotiate the shot via a cushion, and this could easily lead to his making a foul or a mistake. Then you would have an even bigger advantage.

Right: *Many beginners would be tempted to play into the pack. Experience will tell you it is best to roll the cue-ball off a red down the table (below right).*

Below: *The shot to nothing – your opponent's left with a problem!*

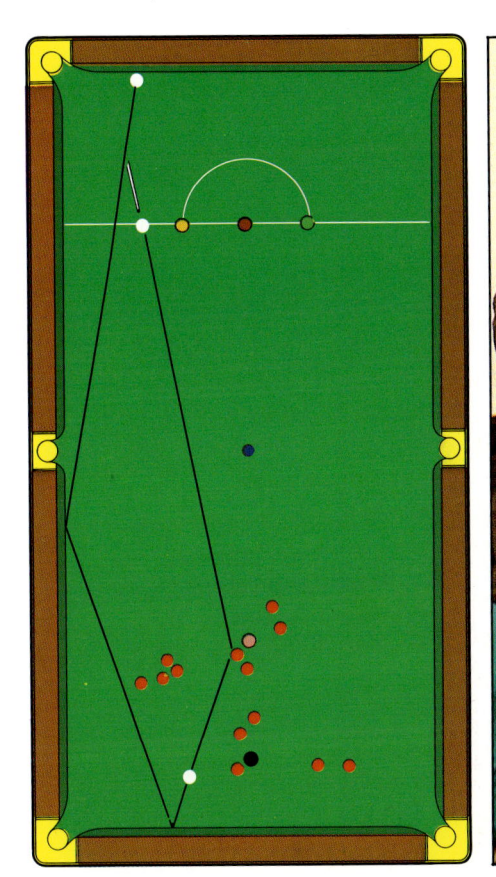

SNOOKERS AND HOW TO ESCAPE

It is very important that you should be able to play snookers. This means that you know how to put your opponent into such a position that he has not got a direct shot at any object ball. If you can play snookers, then your opponent is in trouble, and it often works out to your advantage, as we saw in the last section. But don't forget, it works both ways. You must be able to get out of them, without giving him the advantage.

Most players would be happy merely to hit the object ball after a snooker. If the standard of play of two players is low, then to accomplish that would be enough. But top class players work out what would happen *after* they had hit the object ball. Where will the cue-ball go? Will the opponent be set up for a pot?

Look at the examples below. They show how a beginner and a good player would negotiate a snooker.

> **SNOOKER–IT'S THE NAME OF THE GAME!**
>
> Watching a player get out of a snooker is an impressive sight, but most professionals are capable of getting out of snookers with relative ease. The secret is getting out of them without giving the advantage to your opponent. If you can get out of a snooker by laying a snooker it is generally more by luck than judgement. Laying snookers is an important part of the game – after all that is what the game is called.

It is your experience in learning angles and how side works that helps you to escape from trouble. But not all snookers must be played with the use of the cushions. If there is some distance between the cue-ball and object ball, and there is

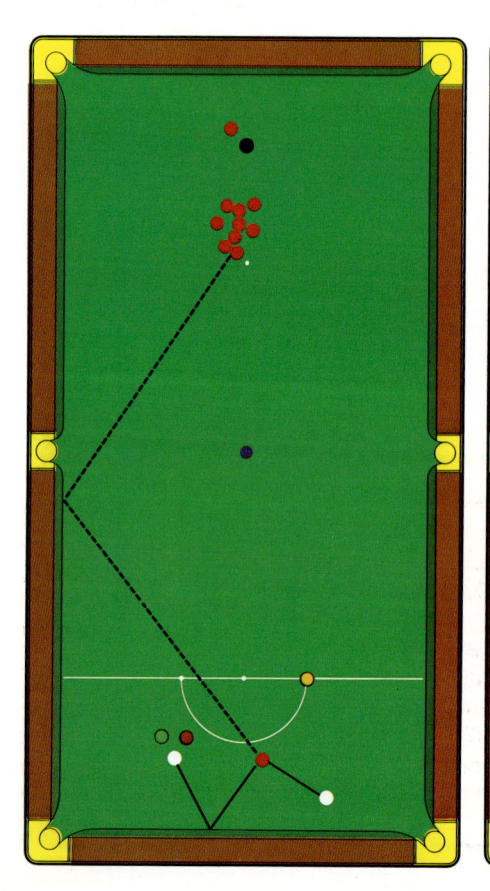

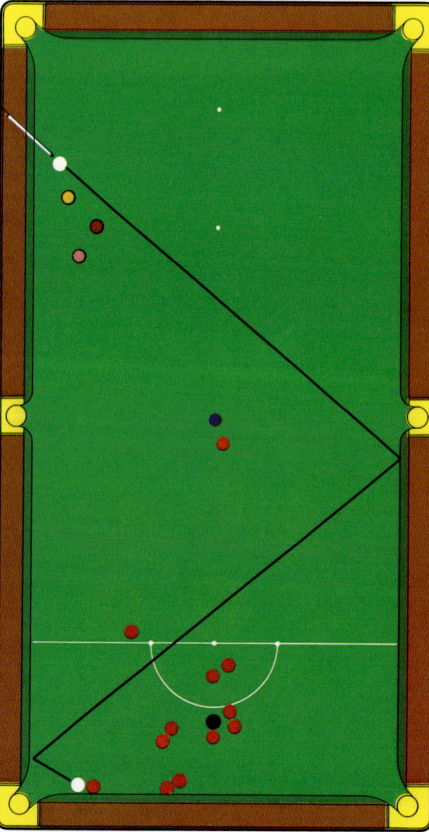

Far left: *laying a snooker. Return the red to the pack and at the same time put your opponent in trouble with a snooker. Stun the white and tuck it up behind the two colours near the bottom cushion.*

Left: *Getting out of a snooker with clever use of two cushions.*

Right: *Not only getting out of a snooker but making the pot as well.*

22

an offending ball in between, you can avoid the snooker by swerving the cue-ball around the offending ball. In order to play the swerve, you must hit down on to the cue-ball, so putting side spin on it.

You must make an attempt to get out of a snooker. If you do not, the referee will penalize you and ask you to play the shot again. Every effort must be made to get out of the snooker.

THE DELIBERATE MISS

You are not allowed to miss deliberately when negotiating a snooker. It is bad sportsmanship and if playing in a match you will be penalized and asked to replay the stroke.

23

TRICK SHOTS

Your friends will be most impressed if you learn some trick shots!

Many professionals have a large collection of trick shots which they perform when they carry out exhibitions. Some are very difficult, but years of practice make them easier than they look. Others, however, are pretty standard and simple, but look effective and clever when carried out.

Here are a couple of trick shots. Both involve potting the black – in a different way.

FIRST TRICK SHOT

This is one of the easiest trick shots to play, but there is no better starting place than here. Position the yellow on the centre spot and in a direct line between it and the centre pocket, position the green, brown, blue and a red ball so they are all touching each other. Position the black near the pocket, and about 3.81 cm (1½ in) from it. The cue-ball should be about 7.62 cm (3 in) from the yellow. Strike the cue-ball in the centre, and fairly hard, so that it makes contact with the yellow. Let the balls do the rest and you will find the black goes into the pocket . . .

SECOND TRICK SHOT

This next one is a bit harder and calls for a little bit more cunning. Position the six reds in an arc as shown, with the last one touching the cushion. The black should

Ask your friends if they think you can make a six-ball plant. If there are any doubters, set the balls up as shown and prove them wrong. You'll have the last laugh . . .

be placed about 3.81 cm (1½ in) from the pocket. This time the cue-ball should be near the middle pocket. When you hit the cue-ball don't hit it too hard. It should be played to the left side of the first red and will roll around the reds, along the cushion and on to the black for another pot.

This second trick shot is a bit harder than the first trick shot, but the feeling of satisfaction when it comes off is great!

If you want to impress your mates that bit more, have a go at this one. Before you try it on them, you want to make sure you have perfected it!

The Professional Game

Until the mid 1920s snooker was regarded as inferior to billiards. There was little skill needed because swerve shots, screw shots and side were not developed. It was primarily a potting game. That all changed with the arrival of Joe Davis (no relation to Steve!) who held the world championship from 1927 until 1946. He brought a new element of skill to the game, and suddenly cue-ball control became as important as potting.

When colour television was introduced in Britain in the 1960s, snooker was opened. Today, anybody can have a game of snooker almost any time of the day.

Sponsors became interested, and so the television companies devoted more viewing hours to the sport. Originally, the BBC covered only the world championships, but now all the major events are covered by BBC and ITV. Lighting was one of the early problems. Often bulbs exploded over the table! Today special lighting equipment is installed, and usually three cameras cover each match.

Jimmy White

Steve Davis

Cliff Thorburn

obviously one of those sports that could benefit. In 1969, BBC television launched its *Pot Black* series and players like Ray Reardon and John Spencer became household names. *Pot Black* played an enormous role in the re-birth of snooker. It has never looked back since that day, and the sport's popularity is still increasing. More people started playing, and more snooker centres were quickly

Some of the giants of snooker. From left to right; Steve Davis, the undisputed number one. Jimmy White, for so long a strong contender for Davis's title. Canada's Cliff Thorburn, a leading player of long-standing. Alex Higgins, twice world champion and the self-styled "People's Champion", Stephen Hendry, the pride of Scotland and the player widely tipped to be Davis's successor. However, the way Davis played in the 1987–88 season, it looks like being a long time before he is dethroned.

THE SNOOKER SEASON

The professional season lasts from September to May, when it ends in England with the game's top tournament, the Embassy World Professional Championship, at Sheffield's Crucible Theatre.

Players are seeded. They receive ranking points throughout the season, and in 1987–88 six events counted as ranking tournaments. The tournaments were: Fidelity Unit Trusts International, Rothmans Grand Prix, Tennents UK Open, Mercantile Credit Classic, MIM Britannia British Open, and Embassy World Championship. The winner of a ranking tournament receives 6 points, the runner-up 5, losing semi-finalist 4, and so on down to the losers in the last 32 who each receive 1 point. However, in the World Championship, more points are at stake, with 10 to the winner and 8 to the runner-up.

In addition to the ranking tournaments there are other events throughout the season, such as: Foster's World Doubles Championship, the Fersina Windows World Team Championship, and the Benson and Hedges Masters.

Because of the large sums of money invested in snooker, players such as Steve Davis, Jimmy White and Dennis Taylor have become some of the highest-paid sportsmen in the UK. In addition to tournament winnings, they are in demand to promote a wide variety of products and so earn a good deal in that way.

Steve Davis has been the most outstanding player since his arrival on the professional snooker scene in 1980, when he beat Alex Higgins to win the Coral UK Championship, his first major win. Since then, Davis has won all the major titles, including the world title on four occasions, and has been at the top of the rankings since 1983.

Davis is still Number 1, but youngsters like Stephen Hendry and Martin Clark are all aiming for the top. And Jimmy White, known as "The Whirlwind" for his quick play, is still hoping to take over at the head of the world rankings.

Alex Higgins

Stephen Hendry

HOW TO PLAY BILLIARDS

Billiards began long before snooker. Originally an outdoor game, the green baize used on tables today is meant to look like grass! You play with only three balls, a red and two whites (one with two black spots called "spot white").

SCORING

Unlike snooker, where you can only score points by potting an object ball (a red or a colour), you have extra chances in billiards of potting either of the other two balls, or even going in-off one of the balls. You can also score points by making a cannon: playing your ball so that it makes contact with the other two.

Points are added to your score as you play each scoring stroke, and a break comes to an end if you fail to score, or commit a foul. A game lasts until one player reaches an agreed number of points, or when time has run out.

If you pot the red, it is brought back on to the table and placed on the spot the black would occupy in snooker. However, if you pot two successive reds from its spot, without making another scoring shot in between, then next time the red has to be spotted on the centre spot (the one normally occupied by the blue in snooker).

If your own ball goes in the pocket, it is brought back into play and played from the "D". All balls played from the "D", either at the start of a game or when a ball is being brought back into play, must be played out of the baulk area and up the table towards the top cushion.

If your opponent's ball enters a pocket, it stays off the table until your break comes to an end. He then plays from the "D". If his ball is off the table, and you cannot pot the red, or go in-off, it is a good idea to try to get your white and/or the red into the baulk area, because as we've said your opponent has to play up the table. You will therefore make his

Billiards, like snooker, is generally played as singles, although it is possible to play in pairs. It's a game of great skill, and knowledge of angles is vitally important.

shot that much harder.

All scoring shots as a result of one stroke count. For example, if you made a cannon and then potted one, or even all of the balls, all scoring strokes would be counted. The maximum score from one stroke is 10.

THE VALUES OF THE SCORING SHOTS

Potting the red .... 3 points
Your ball going in-off the red .... 3 points
Potting your opponent's white .... 2 points
Your ball going in-off your ....
 opponent's .... 2 points
A cannon .... 2 points

If a ball goes in-off after a cannon, the value of the shot depends on which ball your white hit first. If the red, it is worth 5 points, but if it hits your opponent's ball first, it is worth only 4 points.

All fouls carry a two-point penalty, which is added to your opponent's score.

The cannon is one of the most widely used shots in billiards. To play a cannon successfully your cue-ball must strike the two other balls. It's worth two points.

After a foul, the player who plays next can either play the balls as they come to rest, or have the red spotted on its spot (the black in snooker), and his opponent's white on the centre spot. Play then re-starts by playing from the "D". This does not apply, however, if a player is re-starting play from the "D" and both other balls are in the baulk area. He can play a deliberate miss and forfeit two points, but the next player does not have the option to have the balls re-spotted.

How to Play Pool

There are many varieties of pool but one of the most popular forms is 8-Ball Pool.

THE TABLE AND BALLS

The game is played on a much smaller table than billiards and snooker. Tables vary in size considerably, but the majority are 1.83 m (6 ft) by 0.91 m (3 ft). The pockets are different from those on a snooker table, and do not have "string bags" to collect the balls, but are solid.

The table is marked with only one spot, and it is on that spot that the black ball should be placed. The line drawn across the table is known as the string line (remember, it was the baulk line in billiards and snooker), and there is a "D" drawn from the centre of the string line. When beginning or re-starting a game, the white is played from anywhere in the "D", just as in billiards and snooker.

A set of pool balls theoretically consists of seven plain balls of different colours and seven striped balls, also different

This player is obviously on "spots". When he has potted all seven he must pot the black. Some rules stipulate that you must nominate which pocket you put the black into.

There are many ways the balls can be racked at the start of the game. The above is just one example, but different areas of the country have their own variations.

colours, one black ball and a white cue-ball. The 15 coloured balls are all numbered, and the black is No. 8 – hence the name "8-Ball Pool". These days many sets consist of seven plain yellow, and seven plain red balls which are not numbered, because the numbering has no significance in the game of 8-Ball Pool.

THE AIM OF THE GAME

The object is to pot all balls of your colour and then finally pot the black. The first person to do that is the winner. If you pot the black at any other stage of the game, you lose the game. However, if the black goes in from the initial break, the balls are re-spotted and you start again. When making the initial break at least two balls from the pack must hit a cushion for the break to be legal.

The first person to pot a ball then plays on those colours. The other player has the other colours. If you pot two or more balls of a different colour from the break, you can nominate which you want or just carry on playing as if none had gone down until you pot another ball. In that case the colour of that ball potted will determine which ones you play with. Your

If No. 13 is potted, the white may well be left covering the pocket. An excellent snooker!

break continues until you fail to pot a ball or commit a foul.

FOULS

Missing a ball, causing the cue-ball to hit first one of your opponent's balls or the black ball, allowing the white to go into the pocket, or forcing a ball off the table, are all common types of foul. After every foul, your opponent has two shots, but with the first he has what is called a "free table". That means he can hit any ball on the table, even one of yours, or even the black. He can pot one of your balls if he wants (but mustn't pot the black). If after a foul you don't pot a ball with your first shot, you still have another shot. If you miss, then it is your opponent's turn to play. If you pot a ball with the first shot after a foul, you still have at least two more shots.

If you are snookered after a foul shot you can play the ball out of the "D" if you wish, but must ask the referee first.

If your only ball left is the black, and you pot it, and then put the white in the pocket, you lose the game.

PERFECTING YOUR GAME

Safety play, as well as the ability to pot, makes a good pool player. If you delicately place your ball over the pocket (but not in it) your opponent cannot pot a ball in that pocket. So, it is not a disappointment when you leave a pot over the pocket as it is in snooker.

On the other hand, if you pot all your seven balls straight off and your opponent has all seven of his left it does not mean you are winning! In fact it means he will pot one of his balls, and then snooker you in the hope you will play a foul, and give him a free shot.

These are the usual rules of pool, but they do vary throughout the world. You should check in your area which rules are in force.

Index

Angle, 10–11, 22
Accessories, 12

Baulk area, 3, 20–1, 28–9
Billiards, 2, 26
　how to play, 28
Black ball, 2, 4, 8–9, 16–17, 19, 24, 29, 31
Blue ball, 2, 24, 28
Break, 4
Breaking off, 4, 20
Bridge, 7, 9–10, 12–14
Brown ball, 2, 24

Cannon, 28–9
Chalk, 2, 4, 13
Clark, Martin, 27
Coral UK Championship, 27
Cross-rest, 4–5, 13
Cue, 2–3, 6–9
　ball, 2, 4, 6–14, 18–21
　extension, 4
　holding, 6

"D", 3–5, 28–31
Davis, Joe, 2, 16, 26
Davis, Steve, 6, 14, 26
Double, 18, 19

Extended spider, 4

Fine-cut shot, 11
Foul, 4–5, 13, 23, 28, 31
"Free table", 31

Green ball, 2, 17
Grip, 6

Half-ball shot, 10
Half-butt (or long rest), 4, 13
Hendry, Stephen, 26–7
Higgins, Alex, 14, 26–7

"Kiss", 18

Long rest, 4, 13

Object ball, 8–11, 13–15, 18, 22

Pink ball, 2
Plant (or set), 18–19
Pool, how to play, 30–1
Pot Black series, 26

Quarter-ball shot, 11

Reardon, Ray, 26
Red ball, 4–5, 8–9, 16–17, 19–20, 24, 27–9
Rules of snooker, 4–5

Safety shot, 12, 19–20
Scoring, snooker, 3–5
　billiards, 28
　pool, 30–1
Screw, 14–16
Season, professional, 26
Sheffield Crucible Theatre, 27
"Shot to Nothing", 20–1
Side, 14–15, 17, 23
Sighting, 8–9
Snookers, 21–23, 31
Spencer, John, 26
Spider, 3–5, 13
Spin, 14–15, 23
Stance, 7

Table, 2–4
Taylor, Dennis, 27
Thorburn, Cliff, 26
Three-quarter ball shot, 11
Trick shots, 24–5

"V", 7, 12

White, Jimmy, 14, 26–7
World Championship, 27

Yellow ball, 2, 4, 24, 30

Published in 1988 by
The Hamlyn Publishing Group Limited
a division of Paul Hamlyn Publishing
Michelin House, 81 Fulham Road, London SW3 6RB

Copyright © The Hamlyn Publishing Group Limited 1988

All rights reserved. No part of this publication may be reproduced, stored in a retrieval system, or transmitted, in any form or by any means, electronic, mechanical, photocopying, recording or otherwise, without the prior permission of The Hamlyn Publishing Group Limited.

ISBN 0 600 55738 3

Printed and bound in Italy
Front jacket illustration: David Muscroft Photography
Illustrations: Karel Feuerstein
Photographic acknowledgments: David Muscroft Photography
Design: Bob Burroughs
General editors: Gillian Denton, Lynne Williams

The publishers would like to thank Barry White for his invaluable help.